Department of Health

The Quality of Medical Care

Report of the Standing Medical Advisory Committee
for
the Secretaries of State for Health and Wales

London: HMSO

First published 1990

ISBN 0 11 321328 X

Contents

Page		
1	1	INTRODUCTION
1		1.2 Scope of report
1		1.4 Definition and purpose of medical audit
2	2	KEY POINTS AND RECOMMENDATIONS
7	3	HISTORICAL PERSPECTIVE
9	4	GENERAL PRINCIPLES OF MEDICAL AUDIT
10	5	THE CONTEXT OF MEDICAL AUDIT
12	6	VALUE OF MEDICAL AUDIT
14	7	PRACTICE OF MEDICAL AUDIT
14		7.1 Types of medical audit
14		7.2 Practical approach to medical audit
16	8	STEPS TO BE TAKEN TO ESTABLISH MEDICAL AUDIT
16		8.1 General
16		8.2 Medical staff organisation
18		8.3 Resources
19		8.4 Training for medical audit
20		8.5 Confidentiality
20	9	THE CONDUCT OF MEDICAL AUDIT IN DIFFERENT SETTINGS
20		9.1 Medical audit in hospital
25		9.2 Quality in public health medicine
26		9.3 Medical audit in primary care
30		9.4 Medical audit in the private sector

Page

31 10 OUTCOME INDICATORS

33 REFERENCES

35 APPENDIX

1 INTRODUCTION

1.1 The Secretary of State has sought the views of the Standing Medical Advisory Committee on how the quality of medical care may best be assessed and assured in a systematic way. In particular advice was welcomed on:

- types of audit, who should conduct them and how they should be organised and evaluated
- what steps need to be taken to ensure that participation in medical audit, or other appropriate quality assurance assessments, becomes an expected part of routine professional practice
- appropriate approaches to the problem of doctors who decline to participate in such assessments, or whose clinical results fall short of what could reasonably be expected
- the development of a more comprehensive range of indicators of clinical outcome, to cover the full range of medical work.

Scope of the report

1.2 The term 'quality of care' is an all-embracing term which encompasses everything from the patient's call to the receptionist, through the comfort of the waiting room, the effectiveness of appointment systems, the response to complaints, the nutritional quality of hospital food to clinical outcome. Some of these and other aspects of medical care are the responsibility of doctors and should be subject to monitoring and revision. However this report is concerned solely with medical care as provided by the medical profession, in particular with what is commonly referred to as 'medical audit'. The report is not intended to be a handbook of medical audit but aims to set out the principles and framework upon which medical audit activities should be based

1.3 The membership of the Working Group which compiled this report is listed in Appendix 1.

Definition and purpose of medical audit

1.4 There are several definitions of medical audit but we have accepted that given in the recently published NHS Review White Paper[1]:—

'Medical audit can be defined as the systematic, critical analysis of the quality of medical care, including the procedures used for diagnosis and treatment, the use of resources, and the resulting outcome and quality of life for the patient.'

1.5 The term 'clinical audit' has been used to embrace the activities of all health care professionals who work directly with patients, such as nurses, doctors and paramedical staff. In this report the term 'medical audit' refers to the assessment by peer review of medical care provided by the medical profession. It should be acknowledged, however, that the quality of medical care is not solely determined by doctors, as other health professionals also have an essential role: Therefore the role of other health professionals will inevitably come under consideration in 'clinical' audit, particularly as the integrated team approach to patient care is so important in modern medicine.

1.6 The objective of medical audit is to improve the quality of care doctors provide for their patients. Medical audit is an essential component of quality assurance of health care. Quality assurance is a system by which provision or performance is measured against expectation with the declared intention of minimising deficiencies. Medical audit provides a systematic approach to peer review of medical care. Its content is primarily clinical and educational as opposed to managerial and its focus is on the process and outcome of medical care. However where deficiencies in care can be attributed to lack of resources it necessarily impinges on resource provision and financial audit.

2 KEY POINTS AND RECOMMENDATIONS

The key recommendations are reproduced here as set out in the body of the report.

Objectives

2.1 The objective of medical audit is to improve the quality of care doctors provide for their patients (para 1.6).

2.2 The 'grand round' or 'interesting case' type of clinical meeting does *not* meet the requirements of medical audit. Medical audit is a systematic structured procedure with the express purpose of improving the quality of medical care.

Wherever possible it should be quantified (para 4.2).

2.3 Medical audit should lead to changes in the organisation and availability of services, clinical policy and clinical practice with consequent improvement in the quality of medical care as measured by appropriate indicators (para 7.2.1).

Obligations of doctors

2.4 Medical audit is now increasingly recognised as a component of medical practice and therefore all doctors should be expected to take part (para 7.2.1).

2.5 The Working Party felt that taking part in medical audit was such an important component of medical practice in modern health care that a failure to take part should be regarded very seriously. Not only do we feel that such a failure is less than good practice but we feel that there should be overall agreement within the profession about what procedures should be followed if a doctor fails to take part (para 7.2.4).

2.6 If the doctor still fails to take part we feel that it is for the responsible bodies representative of the medical profession such as the Colleges of the various branches of medicine to advise on what peer review mechanism could be helpful in such a situation as we feel very strongly that dealing with this matter should be kept within the professional body. A similar approach would also be needed for those doctors whose clinical results fell persistently short of what would be generally regarded as acceptable. We would suggest therefore that the Colleges should be asked to advise on possible procedures. We hope that the problem of refusal will be most uncommon as the commitment to take part in medical audit is included in future job descriptions (para 7.2.4).

2.7 Medical audit must be an educational process, and this form of audit should not be used for disciplinary purposes (para 8.1.3).

2.8 We believe that medical audit should be considered as part of normal clinical practice; therefore all doctors, whether in the NHS or in the private sector, should participate in a properly structured medical audit programme (para 9.4.1).

Conduct of medical audit

2.9 Medical audit should lead to action where practice has not matched the agreed standards so that the quality of medical care is improved (para 4.1).

2.10 New knowledge, and changing attitudes to disease, handicap or death, constantly generates new approaches to diagnosis and treatment which challenge established practice. Medical audit needs to take into account this new knowledge otherwise it is at risk of fossilising the best of today's medicine in its present phase of development (para 5.1).

2.11 Judgement of method [of investigation and treatment] is best conducted in a spirit of enquiry and with open debate in which dogma is regularly challenged and participants are willing to revise agreed practices (para 5.6).

2.12 The Royal Colleges, their Faculties together with other responsible bodies including clinical associations or societies have an essential role in developing appropriate criteria (para 7.1.1).

2.13 Follow-up action is an absolutely essential feature of medical audit without which the justification for medical audit is lost (para 7.2.1).

2.14 We hope that the use of the autopsy will be encouraged as it remains a relevant final investigation of considerable value in medical audit (para 9.1.12).

2.15 Recommendations for action should be explicit and should be directed to those responsible for their implementation. A record of the audit meetings should be made including the names of all those who attended. The matters discussed, decisions made and the identity of both doctors and patients should be recorded in such a way as to maintain anonymity (para 7.2.3).

Assessment of patient care and medical audit

2.16 It is our belief that while medical audit is unlikely to lead to a short-term dramatic improvement in the quality of medical care we expect more widespread medical audit to improve the quality of care provided by those whose practice would be considered generally to be less than satisfactory, lead to greater consistency in the quality of care provided overall and encourage those doctors currently regarded as 'good' or 'acceptable' to strive to provide even better care (para 6.5).

2.17 Ideally the quality of medical practice should be judged by its outcome (para 5.3).

2.18 Measurement of outcome is most profitable in studying common conditions and procedures in which special care has been taken to ensure complete and reliable recording of data (para 5.4).

2.19 The determination of outcome will often require information about progress of patients whether after discharge from hospital or following treatment in the community. It will be essential to have mechanisms which facilitate follow-up of patients. This could be achieved through the more assiduous use of the NHS number which is currently used on all general practitioners records and may feature on many personal health records (para 10.7).

Organisation of medical audit

2.20 The essential requirements for the establishment of medical audit are an appropriate organisational framework, resources, training and trust, including confidentiality, to underpin it (para 8.1.1).

2.21 We consider that for the successful conduct of medical audit there should be a Medical Audit Co-ordinator at local level with drive, determination and dedication to the concept of medical audit (para 8.2.1).

2.22 We see medical audit as mainly a local activity and the region's role would therefore be largely a supportive one. It would provide appropriate advice and resources, assist in organising medical audit in supra-district specialties and across districts for those specialties with only one consultant. It would facilitate collaborative audit between the hospital and community health services and primary care. In addition regions will have a role in providing educational and experience opportunities both to doctors who are enthusiastic and wish to develop innovative procedures and for those doctors who are reactionary and who are personally disinclined to be involved in audit (para 8.2.2).

2.23 Consultants in public health medicine have a particular duty to advise on the health status of the population and to report annually. Their specialist training in epidemiology and statistics provides a valuable resource for clinical colleagues undertaking medical audit (para 9.2.1).

Training

2.24 An understanding of the principles of medical audit must become an established part of undergraduate and postgraduate medical education (para 5.6).

2.25 It is important that all doctors should understand medical audit. Education should therefore be offered on a local basis to all GPs and hospital doctors, provided by professional peers teaching by example, with the support of Health Authorities, Postgraduate Deans, Clinical Tutors and College Tutors (para 8.4.1).

We see a need for the collection of information on medical audit and its dissemination to the medical profession as a whole on a regular basis perhaps by means of an 'Audit Magazine' (para 8.4.4).

2.26 Medical schools should be encouraged to inculcate a self-critical approach to medical method and practice throughout the curriculum. Clinical firms to which medical students are attached should be expected to demonstrate good clinical practice in all areas including medical audit. Regional Postgraduate Deans should be expected to recommend disallowance of pre-registration House Officer posts in which medical audit is not an integral part of routine practice (para 8.4.3).

2.27 Training will also need to be provided for medical audit assistants who are likely to be recruited from the ranks of nurses, medical records staff and medical secretaries (para 8.3.2).

Resources

2.28 The effective conduct of medical audit has important resource implications, particularly in terms of medical and other staff manpower and information technology (para 8.3.1).

2.29 Time will need to be set aside on a regular basis for doctors to meet. The time required will of course depend on length and frequency of meetings. We consider that doctors should meet at least once a month. Since all doctors are expected to take part the total time needed which would otherwise be used in direct patient care could be substantial (para 8.3.2).

Confidentiality

2.30 Confidentiality is essential. We recommend therefore that the documentation of audit meetings are provided in an appropriately anonymised form so that the general conclusions of the meeting and recommended action are recorded while the cases used in the discussion are not in any way identifiable (para 8.5.2).

Private hospitals

2.31 We do not consider it appropriate that legislation be introduced requiring the private sector to have medical audit in place, as this would go against the essential nature of medical audit as an educational tool in which doctors should take part in a spirit of enquiry and could lead to formal, rigid protocols or procedures in a field where judgement is required (para 9.4.2).

2.32 We recommend that all NHS contracts placed with the private sector will include a requirement that full and effective medical audit systems are in place (para 9.4.2).

3 HISTORICAL PERSPECTIVE

3.1 The idea of medical audit is not new: indeed, reference to it can be found in the Charter of the Royal College of Physicians of 1518 which states that one of the College's functions is to uphold the standards of medicine 'both for their own honour and public benefit'. Examples of medical audit which are currently taking place include the Confidential Enquiry into Maternal Deaths, which began in 1952 and is run jointly by the Department of Health and the Royal College of Obstetricians and Gynaecologists[2]. The Royal College of General Practitioners was involved early on in medical audit in general practice. Much of the work of the Birmingham Research Unit in the 1950's and 1960's was concerned with designing the tools for audit. In pathology the National External Quality Assessment Scheme (NEQAS) was started in 1969 and encompasses all commonly used numerical investigations in pathology. It is a voluntary scheme open to NHS and private services. The Royal College of Physicians conducted a survey in 1980 of causes of death in medical wards of all patients under the age of 50. The Association of Anaesthetists and the Association of Surgeons together carried out an enquiry into perioperative deaths in three Regions (CEPOD)[4]; this was extended into a national confidential enquiry at the beginning of 1989. The Health Advisory Service, which was established in 1976, is an example of multidisciplinary audit; it carries out reviews of hospitals and community health services provided for the elderly and the mentally ill and makes recommendations for the improvement of care.

3.2 The Department of Health's health service indicators include measures of activity, and some of outcome including stillbirth rates, neonatal mortality rates, low birthweight rates, postneonatal mortality rates, perinatal mortality rates, immunisation rates and infectious disease notification rates. These provide some indication of the quality of medical care. The health service indicators also include a set of data which compares death rates by region and district for certified causes of death from conditions considered 'potentially avoidable' such as asthma, tuberculosis, hypertension, cerebrovascular disease and cancer of the cervix. The incidence of potentially avoidable deaths (that is those from conditions amenable to treatment) has been analyzed for each Health Authority and shows large variations between Health Authorities even after adjustment for social factors. All these may provide some indication of the quality of medical care.

3.3 The move is now to match these separate initiatives by developing systems for the overall consideration of care by individual doctors. There is increasing acceptance by the medical profession that the work of a doctor should be examined against a background of currently agreed good practice while allowing flexibility for evolution in what is perceived to be good practice. The Royal Colleges and their Faculties have always taken considerable interest in the principle of medical audit and increasingly seek evidence of functioning audit before accrediting posts for specialist training. The Royal College of General Practitioners launched its Quality Initiative in 1983[5], essentially an initiative in medical audit, and in introduced a new system for entry to its Fellowship, based on performance-based assessment in the practice. Other Colleges have convened working parties and run seminars to define and disseminate medical audit and this has led to a number of publications and reports[3,6].

3.4 The demands for the provision of health care are potentially unbounded and continue to increase as a result of factors such as ageing of the population and advances in medical technology. It is important therefore that the most appropriate use of resources is made in the treatment of patients. This can only be achieved through careful examination by the medical profession of its own practices. The profession has a responsibility to society, from which it derives its authorisation and economic support, to practice its skills prudently and to be increasingly involved in deciding priorities for medical care of the population.

4 GENERAL PRINCIPLES OF MEDICAL AUDIT

4.1 The essential nature of medical audit is a frank discussion between doctors, on a regular basis and without fear of criticism, of the quality of care provided as judged against agreed standards but in a context which allows evolutionary change in such standards. It should lead to action where practice has not matched the agreed standards so that the quality of medical care is improved. The principles of medical audit can be compared with those of feed back loop control in which the expected standard of care is defined in whatever terms are agreed to be appropriate, reality is compared with the defined standard and practice is changed in the light of this comparison. This is referred to as the 'audit cycle'[3].

4.2 Although sharing similar objectives with medical audit in respect of medical education and training, the 'grand round' or 'interesting case' type of clinical meeting does not meet the requirements of medical audit. Medical audit is a systematic structured procedure with the express purpose of improving the quality of medical care. Wherever possible it should be quantified.

4.3 Medical care can be considered in terms of structure, process or outcome[7]. Structure is concerned with the amount and type of resources available, for example the condition of buildings, the number of beds available and staffing levels. These are easy to measure but are not necessarily good indicators of the quality of care provided. Process relates to the amount and type of activity expended in the care of a patient. Unless resources are severely limited process has more significance than structure and in many circumstances it is the only measure available. The most relevant indicator of quality of care is outcome. Some outcomes may be difficult to measure since the final outcome may not be evident until many years later. Examples of outcome measures include mortality, such as perinatal mortality and perioperative deaths, residual disability, relief of symptoms and patient satisfaction. This is discussed more fully in Section 10.

5 THE CONTEXT OF MEDICAL AUDIT

5.1 In its commercial context 'audit' describes the assessment of an institution's financial procedures against best practices. Adopting the term as a metaphor in medicine implies that there are agreed best practices and easily measured outputs in medicine; these implications are only partially true. New knowledge, and changing attitudes to disease, handicap or death, constantly generates new approaches to diagnosis and treatment which challenge established practice. Medical audit needs to take into account new knowledge and attitudes otherwise it is at risk of fossilising the best of today's medicine in its present phase of development.

5.2 Ideally medical advances (this would include amongst other things developments in drugs, surgery, advice on behaviour, counselling and in the use and membership of the caring team) should be tested within accepted ethical principles in controlled trials. However, this is not always possible. Some affect diseases that are too rare; others are too operator-dependent for the results of trials to be generally applicable. Controlled trials can only answer one question, or a few questions, at a time and are conducted on clearly defined groups, so that care must be taken in extending their results to unselected patients with the same disease as seen in medical practice. They can be very expensive in time and resources. The accelerating expansion of biological knowledge is producing new agents faster than they can be fully tested over the range of doses, and in the varied combinations, that are required. These problems are further magnified when long term outcome is considered. Consequently it is not always possible to lay down hard and fast rules that all doctors should follow. Much of medical practice in the treatment of individual patients will continue to depend on judgement of the balance of probabilities. Nevertheless rather than the problems of controlled trials making medical audit difficult they do in fact increase the importance of properly designed and supported medical audit.

5.3 Ideally the quality of medical practice should be judged by its outcome. However there are several major difficulties in relying entirely on judgement of outcome.

5.3.1 Inadequacy of data

There is an understandable anxiety in the medical profession that judgements will be made on the basis of erroneous or incomplete information. We stress the need for information on the type of patient treated as well as the outcome before valid conclusions can be drawn. Quite small differences between patient populations can make big differences to the outcome of treatment. Consequently the results of one hospital in treating a condition can be judged against national or regional averages only if the characteristics of the patients attending that hospital and others in the country or region are known.

5.3.2 Changes in the patient population and treatments available

To make valid judgements about small changes in outcome one needs a stable population and unchanging methods of treatment; these are achievable for a limited time in controlled trials but they seldom pertain in clinical practice. Small or even large changes in outcome may reflect changes in referral practice or selection of patients. For this reason any audit results which are not related to a population base should be treated with circumspection. Similarly audit of a unit's work requires attention to outcome for non-attenders. Failure to include them may lead to a unit overrating or underrating the success of current work practices.

5.3.3 Sample size

Chance variations in outcome from year to year will often obscure small but important changes in outcome particularly in less common conditions. Using longer periods of observation may delay remedial action and spread the study over a time scale in which changes in patient population and type of treatment must be taken into account. The extent of this problem is not sufficiently recognised. For instance if a major operation has a mortality of 1% a rise in mortality to 2% would be a cause for great concern. However if the hospital performs the operation 100 times a year a shift from 1 to 2 deaths will often occur by chance in one year. Such an increase would have a high (95%) chance of indicating a true rise in mortality to 2% only if it occurred for 6 years in succession.

5.4 Consequently measurement of outcome is most profitable in studying common conditions and procedures in which special care has been taken to ensure complete and reliable recording of data. This is not a practicable approach for the whole of a hospital or practice's activities. However the discipline of achieving higher standards with common conditions is likely to be reflected across the rest of care.

5.5 Nevertheless outcome analysis can be of value in monitoring day to day clinical practice. A major change in work done or in outcome may be spotted by watching the quarterly or annual figures at an early stage. Being alert to the possibility that a jump in mortality or morbidity may be due to more than chance variation allows early investigation and intervention. Such investigation must always be in a spirit of scientific enquiry without prejudgement.

5.6 Because outcome measurement has so many limitations in practice, much of medical audit is at present an examination of the methods of investigation and treatment employed. Implicit in this approach is a belief that choosing an approved method will result in a better outcome; often this belief will be based on sensible reasoning but not on established fact. Judgement of method is best conducted in a spirit of enquiry and with open debate in which dogma is regularly challenged and participants are willing to revise agreed practices. An understanding of the principles of medical audit must become an established part of undergraduate and postgraduate medical education.

6 VALUE OF MEDICAL AUDIT

6.1 Since medical audit is essentially a professional activity based on judgements made of the quality of care given to individual patients, or groups of similar patients, the details must necessarily remain confidential and much of the work of audit which has been undertaken remains unpublished. However, there are a number of examples both in the UK and elsewhere of the ways in which the practice of medical audit has led to improvements in clinical care and resource use.

6.2 It is generally accepted by the medical profession that medical audit can improve the appropriateness and adequacy of clinical care. In addition to improving the quality of care for individual patients medical audit can be used to identify diagnostic and treatment procedures that are of little or no benefit so that the resources used in these less effective and often inappropriate procedures can then be diverted to other purposes. Several studies have demonstrated the value of medical audit in reducing the number of unnecessary diagnostic tests performed, length of stay and the number of drugs prescribed[8,9].

6.3 Several studies in general practice have shown that performance in a number of areas can be improved by peer review including management of common clinical conditions, record keeping, prescribing, and referral practices[11,12]. The greatest changes occurred in the behaviour of those doctors whose performance was furthest from from 'optimal' on the criteria used.

6.4 The results of the first five years of a programme of medical audit involving the 31 general surgeons and urologists working in the Lothian Health Board showed statistically significant improvements in some clinical practices including a fall in the number of reoperations and a reduction in deaths associated with a range of surgical operations. Early audit data showed the results of arterial surgery were better in units with surgeons who specialised in vascular surgery[13]. This led to vascular cases being dealt with by a specialised unit and it is believed that this was partly responsible for the reduction in deaths and reoperations. Similarly it has been shown that the success rate in a surgical unit for the surgical treatment of biliary atresia is very dependent on the number of operations done[14,15]. Reductions in wound infection rates have been linked to medical audit[16]. These improvements were linked to reductions in length of stay and hence released resources for use elsewhere.

6.5 It is therefore our belief that while medical audit is unlikely to lead to a short-term dramatic improvement in the quality of medical care we expect more widespread medical audit to improve the quality of care provided by those whose practice would be considered generally to be less than satisfactory, lead to greater consistency in the quality of care provided overall and encourage those doctors currently regarded as 'good' or 'acceptable' to strive to provide even better care. What evidence there is indicates that important improvements both in medical care and in the use of resources can be made.

7 PRACTICE OF MEDICAL AUDIT

7.1 **Types of medical audit**

7.1.1 There are two main approaches to the practice of medical audit. They are (i) retrospective internal audit within a specialty, hospital, general practice or district community in which records are used to review past events, and (ii) concurrent audit which is a continuous assessment of patient management. In both types of audit results are compared with agreed standards, which may be implicit or explicit, protocols or criteria. We feel that retrospective internal audit is likely to be the most appropriate approach for the introduction of medical audit but these approaches to audit are not mutually exclusive. The Royal Colleges, their Faculties together with other responsible bodies including clinical associations or societies have an essential role in developing appropriate standards and criteria.

7.1.2 Ideally the basis of audit should be outcome but in practice it is often not. Usually audit of 'process' is carried out on the assumption that good process gives rise to good outcome. The subject of audit may include administrative processes (such as medical records, referral and discharge letters), clinical processes (use of drugs, investigations and procedures), clinical condition (classified by diagnostic category) or outcome (return to work, ambulation or unexpected death).

7.2 **Practical approach to medical audit**

7.2.1 Medical audit is now increasingly recognised as a component of medical practice and therefore all doctors should be expected to take part. The main components in the process are:

- identification of subject matter to be assessed
- establishment of suitable criteria agreed locally against which to judge performance. Criteria should be based on the best published figures

where available or on criteria provided by the Royal Colleges or other appropriate group if such criteria exist
- identification and analysis of any problems
- refining the above criteria in the light of experience
- formulation of recommendations and follow-up action

Follow-up action is an absolutely essential feature of medical audit without which the justification for medical audit is lost. Medical audit should lead to changes in the organisation and availability of services, clinical policy and clinical practice with consequent improvement in the quality of medical care as measured by appropriate indicators.

7.2.2 Clinical firms and general practices may wish to draw up a programme of work on a yearly basis. Decisions will need to be made on the choice of subject, objectives to be attained, the number of patients to be reviewed, how they should be selected (randomly or systematically and by what criteria) and the time period to be covered.

7.2.3 Recommendations for action should be explicit and should be directed to those responsible for their implementation. A record of the audit meetings should be made including the names of all those who attended. The matters discussed, decisions made and the identity of both doctors and patients should be recorded in such a way as to maintain anonymity.

7.2.4 The Working Party felt that taking part in medical audit was such an important component of medical practice in modern health care that a failure to take part should be regarded very seriously. Not only do we feel that such a failure is less than good practice but we feel that there should be overall agreement within the profession about what procedures should be followed if a doctor fails to take part. Initially this would be dealt with at a local level through informal discussion between the Medical Audit Coordinator, the Head of the appropriate department and the doctor concerned. If the doctor persisted in his or her failure then a somewhat more formal interview with the doctor should be arranged again at a local level involving the appropriate senior members of the consultant committee/medical advisory committee. If the doctor still fails to take part we feel that it is for the responsible bodies representative of the medical profession such as the Colleges of the various branches of medicine to advise on what peer review mechanism could be helpful in such a situation as we feel very strongly that dealing with this matter should be kept within the professional body. A similar approach would also be needed for those doctors whose clinical results fell persistently short of what would be generally regarded as acceptable. We would suggest therefore that the Colleges should be asked to advise on possible procedures. We hope that the problem of refusal will be most uncommon as the commitment to take part in medical audit will be included in future job descriptions.

8 STEPS TO BE TAKEN TO ESTABLISH MEDICAL AUDIT

8.1 **General**

8.1.1 The essential requirements for the establishment of medical audit are an appropriate organisational framework, resources, training and trust including confidentiality, to underpin it.

8.1.2 Since the technical competence to assess quality of medical care belongs to doctors, medical audit must be conducted by the medical profession as its success depends so much on medical knowledge. Medical audit needs to involve all doctors who should take corporate responsibility for it.

8.1.3 Medical audit should lead to a better standard of patient care by better informed doctors. It must be an educational process, and this form of audit should not be used for disciplinary purposes.

8.2 **Medical staff organisation**

8.2.1 We consider that for the successful conduct of medical audit there should be a Medical Audit Co-ordinator at District or Unit level with drive, determination and dedication to the concept of medical audit. There should be a co-ordinator for the Hospital and Community Health Services and a co-ordinator for the Family Health Services Authority each at local level. The co-ordinator should command the support both of the DHA (or FHSA) and the hospital and community medical staff (or local general practitioners). We would expect the Medical Audit Co-ordinator in the District to be a doctor drawn from the membership of the appropriate Medical Advisory Committee or equivalent body and supported in his or her work by an Audit Subcommittee. (In section 8.3 on primary care this committee has been referred to as the Medical Audit Advisory Group (MAAG). The co-ordinator should have easy access to and have good working relations with the general manager. There should be a clear understanding and acceptance by the DHA, FHSA or its equivalent that the responsibility for medical audit resides with the audit subcommittee of the Medical Advisory Committee or its equivalent. Depending on the demands placed upon the audit co-ordinator he or she may need up to 4–5 sessions per week. The role of Medical Audit Co-ordinator within a District may be undertaken by the District Postgraduate Tutor.

8.2.2 By its nature medical audit is essentially a local activity and the region's role would therefore be largely a supportive one. It would provide appropriate advice and resources, assist in organising medical audit in supra-district specialities and across districts for those specialities with only one consultant. It would facilitate collaborative audit between the hospital and community health services and primary care. In addition regions will have a role in providing educational and experience opportunities both to doctors who are enthusiastic and wish to develop innovative procedures and for those doctors who are reactionary and who are personally disinclined to be involved in audit.

8.2.3 The duties of the co-ordinator should be specified. He/she may need to:

- co-ordinate various specialty groups involved in audit
- liaise between consultants and managers in respect of resources required for audit and implementation of recommendations emerging from medical audit and report in a suitable form to the Health Authority on the implementation of medical audit
- chair the audit subcommittee
- collate information from all sources of audit and make appropriate recommendations
- monitor the action recommended
- monitor statistics including performance indicators
- arrange inter-disciplinary meetings
- promote and support education
- review the literature on medical audit and disseminate it
- give advice when requested on what to audit and how
- liaise closely with the department of post-graduate education, district medical education committee and other bodies

8.2.4 Any Region or Special Health Authority which has within its administrative area a supraregional service should ensure that medical audit takes place within that service. If a district health authority has within its area a hospital which has opted for self-governing status but which contains a supraregional unit the health authority should ensure that the medical audit of its supraregional activities take place. The results of the medical audit should be transmitted through the Region to the Supraregional Service Advisory Group.

8.2.5 FHSA areas vary markedly in size and in the larger ones it may be best to adopt smaller working modules, say at District level, with a Medical Audit Coordinator for each one (further consideration of general practice is given in Section 8.3).

8.2.6 In the light of the NHS Review White Paper we consider that the practice of audit should be perceived to be a provider function (whether NHS Hospital Trust, directly managed hospital or private hospital) and purchasers should be expected to be satisfied that effective audit procedures are in place in institutions with which they lay contracts.

8.3 **Resources**

8.3.1 The effective conduct of medical audit has important resource implications, particularly in terms of medical and other staff manpower and information technology.

Manpower

8.3.2 The quality of medical audit will be directly related to the time available to doctors and the number and calibre of support staff. Training will also need to be provided for medical audit assistants who are likely to be recruited from the ranks of nurses, medical records staff and medical secretaries. Time will need to be set aside on a regular basis for doctors to meet. The time required will of course depend on length and frequency of meetings. We consider that doctors should meet at least once a month. Since all doctors are expected to take part the total time needed which would otherwise be used in direct patient care could be substantial. Estimates of time needed range from 1–4 hours per month for all doctors taking part. Time will also be required for supporting staff such as secretaries and medical records staff.

Information technology

8.3.3 In many clinical areas where medical audit will be expected to start computers will not be available. This does not mean that some form of audit will not be able to take place. However, it is likely to be less than ideal and the need for computers in these areas will become apparent. Where possible existing computer systems should be used. The use of stand alone computer systems which cannot make use of existing patient administration systems (PAS) should be avoided. It is important to ensure that new PAS systems being installed are compatible with carrying out medical audit and are readily accessible to medical (and other) staff. In view of the greater heterogeneity of patient contacts and numbers of patients seen in general practice the need for computers will exist just as much as in hospital but they will not be available in the majority of practices. However we would stress that computers are not absolutely necessary before some form of medical audit can start.

Medical records

8.3.4 Accurate medical records are essential for successful medical audit. The coding of hospital admissions may need to be improved and streamlined to allow use for medical audit. Poor coding may be a reflection of many doctors' present perception of the importance of accurate and timely coding of patient records. Accurate coding of patient records is a fundamental requirement of medical audit. Consultants should ensure that summary sheets are completed properly so that records can be quickly and accurately coded by medical records staff.

8.4 Training for medical audit

8.4.1 It is important that all doctors should understand medical audit. Education should therefore be offered on a local basis to all GPs and hospital doctors, provided by professional peers teaching by example, with the support of Health Authorities, Postgraduate Deans, Clinical Tutors and College Tutors. This is a new high priority and will require resources.

8.4.2 Additional training may need to be given to those responsible for coordinating and organising medical audit including non-medical supporting staff.

8.4.3 Medical schools should be encouraged to inculcate a self-critical approach to medical method and practice throughout the curriculum. Clinical firms to which medical students are attached should be expected to demonstrate good clinical practice in all areas including medical audit. House Officer posts in which medical audit is not an integral part of routine practice should not be approved for pre-registration training.

8.4.4 We see a need for the collection of information on medical audit and its dissemination to the medical profession as a whole on a regular basis perhaps by means of an 'Audit Magazine'.

8.5 **Confidentiality**

8.5.1 In medical audit a patient's clinical records will be open to scrutiny by doctors other than the doctor responsible for the patients' clinical care. This sharing of information is legitimate in that all doctors share the same ethical principles in respect of the confidentiality of patient information. However those organising medical audit sessions should do their utmost to avoid referring to patients' names or revealing information by which patients may be identified. It is possible to conduct medical audit without using patients' names.

8.5.2 Concern has been expressed that any record of the discussions of a medical audit meeting could be subject to legal subpoena. It is important that doctors should not feel that they are under a greater threat of litigation because of their involvement in medical audit. Confidentiality is essential. We recommend therefore that the documentation of audit meetings are provided in an appropriately anonymised form so that the general conclusions of the meeting and recommended action are recorded while the cases used in the discussion are not in any way identifiable.

9 THE CONDUCT OF MEDICAL AUDIT IN DIFFERENT SETTINGS

9.1 **Medical audit in hospital**

9.1.1 Medical audit can be practised in various ways. At a local level most specialty groups would favour regular retrospective reviews of clinical practice. Such meetings are able to review workload as well as clinical outcome, including complications and death. At such meetings deficiencies in facilities or patient care can be identified and recommendations made to effect improvements.

9.1.2 For such meetings to be successful they have to

- take place regularly (at least once a month) at a time set aside from other hospital work. The frequency will depend on the specialty.
- be attended by all relevant medical staff, especially the consultants
- be prepared in advance. Data on clinical activity needs to be compiled and produced for each meeting. Notes of patients to be discussed have to be found.
- be totally confidential. The identity of patients discussed should never be revealed or be capable of being traced.
- be able to make recommendations to management or other appropriate bodies where deficiencies in the service have been identified.

9.1.3 We recommend that medical audit meetings should be instituted in all hospital medical departments. The precise method of audit will be decided by the medical staff concerned, but should be based firmly on the recommendations by the Royal Colleges, Faculties and other groups. Where the same specialty is represented in two or more hospitals in the same health authority audit meetings could be usefully combined. In the same way, specialty groups with similar interests (eg cardiology and cardiac surgery) could hold joint audit meetings. We would expect medical staff in the diagnostic departments (eg radiology and pathology) and the anaesthetic department to be asked to attend audit meetings of other specialties as appropriate. Nonetheless these service specialties will need to conduct audit meetings on their own behalf (see paragraphs 9.1.10–9.1.17). Each specialty group will keep confidential records of their audit meetings. We hope that where appropriate other professionals involved in the care of patients may wish to develop joint auditing initiatives with medical staff.

9.1.4 The Medical Audit Co-ordinator, by occasional attendances at meetings and by receipt of reports, should satisfy himself that effective audit is being carried out in all departments. He will report to the appropriate Medical Advisory Committee or equivalent body and the Health Authority as appropriate.

9.1.5 Although the simplest forms of medical audit can be initiated almost immediately with little extra expense other than the medical time involved, it is doubtful whether such audit could achieve the aim and objectives required of medical audit which is properly organized, namely the expectation that poor practice will be quickly identified and improved.

9.1.6 Departments will soon require computer facilities for compiling data on which the audit is to be based. The computers needed might range from a small desk top unit to a much larger hospital based system capable of providing patient information to all departments undertaking audit. The selection of the type of computer will depend on the unit and the types of audit undertaken. The need for compatibility has already been noted (paragraph 8.3.3). Personnel and training to operate such systems would also be required.

9.1.7 Hospital departments will require help in setting up medical audit for the first time and should seek the help of the Medical Audit Co-ordinator. We hope that full use will be made of the facilities that have been offered by the Royal Colleges and other bodies. We also see a special role for departments of postgraduate medical education in this regard and they should be resourced for the purpose.

9.1.8 Audit should not be allowed to become a burden upon specialty groups as this will reduce participation. Detailed examination of the outcomes of a large number of patients is not practical. Some form of selection, which can be random or systematic but could include certain instructive cases, is required so that time is available for proper discussion of any problems encountered.

9.1.9 The Medical Audit Co-ordinator would be responsible to the medical advisory committee or its equivalent for ensuring that medical audit was established in all hospital medical departments. He or she would tackle 'pockets of resistance' amongst consultants with the support of the medical advisory committee. He or she would need to advise hospital departments and management on computer systems for medical audit, ensuring that such systems are compatible and capable of integration within the hospital as a whole. The Medical Audit Co-ordinator would report to the medical audit committee and medical advisory committee whose responsibility would be to keep management informed. The time spent by the Medical Audit Co-ordinator on carrying out these tasks will vary depending on the size of the hospital concerned and the specialties within it. The Medical Audit Co-ordinator will need to be provided with paid sessions together with appropriate secretarial facilities in order to carry out this work. A recent publication provides useful information on the practice of medical audit in hospitals[17].

Diagnostic departments

9.1.10 The diagnostic specialities of pathology and radiology have their own particular requirements for audit. These include a review of diagnostic accuracy as well as such matters as timeliness and records. They should also include a review of contributions to the general standards of patient care, such as ensuring an appropriate use of investigations or the appropriateness of cross infection studies. Diagnostic accuracy audit should include a review of anonymised random samples of recent investigations by a peer group of the same speciality. Both the Royal College of Pathologists and the Royal College of Radiologists have already made significant contributions to audit and are developing guidelines for local audit.

9.1.11 Proper audit in pathology must take account both of the accuracy required of numerical results and the adequacy demanded of interpretational and clinical work. National schemes are already available for the quality assurance of many pathology investigations including all the commonly performed numerical assays and these should continue. The interpretative and clinical work must also be audited and this is often less suited to the discussion group approach at a hospital level convenient for some other disciplines. The initiative of the Royal College of Pathology in organising an audit and accreditation scheme as a national programme, currently being piloted in one Regional Health Authority, is commended, particularly as unlike other specialities many pathology departments lack trainees and so are not currently visited by the College. The scheme must of course take into account the National External Quality Assessment Scheme (NEQAS) results and, for investigations for which the NEQAS schemes are not applicable, must take into account involvement in locally organised peer review schemes.

9.1.12 Where consultants in radiology and pathology are involved in direct patient care, as for example in oncology, haematology or interventional radiology, the same principles as those described for general medicine or surgery apply. In addition both diagnostic specialities have a role in the audit of the practice of medicine and surgery, and should help in the assessment of the use of investigations, and their interpretation. Similarly appropriate clinical specialties have a role in the audit of pathology and radiology. We hope also that the use of the autopsy will be encouraged as it remains a relevant final investigation of considerable value in medical audit.

Anaesthesia

9.1.13 Anaesthetists like others already have morbidity and mortality meetings the holding of which is one criterion in the College of Anaesthetists' accreditation of training posts. In these meetings individual cases are presented and debated. There is a need for these meetings to be made more comprehensive, involving other relevant disciplines, and also to be directed to the solution of locally perceived problems.

9.1.14 The collection of reports.of critical incidents, as is done by airline pilots, is an important way in which some departments have identified deficiencies in their own structure (such as provision and checks of functional equipment) or process (such as availability of senior support). Many serious problems were revealed in the Survey of Anaesthetic Practice, carried out by the Association of Anaesthetists of Great Britain and Ireland, and these matters must be pursued. This information was acquired by a method which maintained confidentiality.

9.1.15 Other outcomes, such as minor morbidity without prolongation of hospital stay (eg nausea, vomiting, headache, minor bruising) and intermediate morbidity with prolongation of hospital stay (eg post-dural puncture headache, preparation for operation, postoperative pain relief) are all potential indicators of quality. There are other aspects of the work of anaesthetists which need to be audited such as obstetric analgesia, intensive therapy and pain therapy services. These three developments have proceeded at very different rates in different parts of the country and audit of these is required nationally, perhaps by the College of Anaesthetists through its regional representatives.

9.1.16 The development of agreed medical management for a model case by means of discussion by groups of different degrees of experience has started in one region. The protocols which resulted are used as educational tools and are popular. They can also be used in comparison with the management of real cases.

9.1.17 The scrutiny of anaesthetic records is an essential part of audit meetings. This has already resulted in improvements, but considerable financial investment is required in new technology before anaesthetic records can be regarded as satisfactory. It is now possible for routine observations (such as pulse, blood pressure, gas concentrations) to be recorded continuously, automatically and directly on paper. This development is central to any desire for retrospective examination of events during anaesthesia, particularly when rapid physiological changes take place, in order to identify deviations from 'satisfactory' practice.

9.2 **Quality in public health medicine**

9.2.1 The specialty is concerned with the epidemiology of disease, the control of infection, health promotion and the organization and delivery of health services. As community medicine it has undergone repeated evaluations as a specialty, training programmes have been subject to several revisions, posts have been redefined and individuals have faced competitive reappointment. The Government's acceptance of the report of the Public Health Inquiry[18] places the specialty on a firm footing as modern public health medicine and defines the role and and responsibilities of health authorities for the health of the public. Consultants in public health medicine have a particular duty to advise on the health status of the population and to report annually. Their specialist training in epidemiology and statistics provides a valuable resource for clinical colleagues undertaking medical audit. The posts many of them hold will also give them a natural liaison role with management (rather than the representative role mentioned in the NHS Review Working Paper on Medical Audit)[1] and they should be able to assist the development of medical audit in Districts and Regions. Some academic departments may be able to offer specific help and advice.

9.2.2 There is additionally a requirement that the specialty should audit its own practice. The Faculty of Public Health Medicine is developing guidelines for the assistance of its members and fellows. The problems of defining and measuring health outcomes are well known and are even more difficult in public health medicine than in clinical medicine because the specialty is dealing with long-term trends rather than short-term gains. In auditing their own work public health doctors will, like clinical colleagues, incorporate both process and outcome measures. They will also aim to define some measures which will form an acceptable basis for comparative assessment across the country.

9.2.3 The ultimate goal of improvement in the public health is however influenced by many agencies other than health services so it is difficult to measure the specific contribution of the public health practitioner. Many public health doctors work in multi-disciplinary teams committed to integration of their efforts and separating out one group for audit purposes might be counter-productive. It is intended to develop audit in different kinds of departments (single-handed/fully staffed; District/Region; service/academic) in order to study and evaluate various approaches for public health medicine, involving:— peer group review of single events; regular ongoing peer group reviews; performance review/goal attainment; individual and departmental programme review; training review. Some of these types of audit are already being practised and evidence of a satisfactory audit programme is being sought by visiting Specialist Advisory Committee reviews of training posts.

9.2.4 The principles of audit (written records and clear, agreed standards of performance) apply to all types of audit and departments of public health medicine will be expected to join in arrangements which are being made for audit, in the same way as clinical colleagues. The Faculty is offering a regional specialist support structure for audit and is in a position to disseminate the results of pilot studies.

9.2.5 The systems of audit in clinical specialties have been derived in the main from traditional scientific methodologies. Similar approaches can be used in the audit of public health medicine. It is likely, however, that the methodologies of the social sciences will also need to be used and these are less familiar to many doctors. They can have the same scientific rigour, and meet the same criteria for validity, repeatability and reliability as more traditional approaches.

9.3 **Medical audit in primary care**

9.3.1 The Royal College of General practitioners and the General Medical Services Committee, working in association, have an important role both centrally and peripherally in ensuring the success of medical audit in general practice.

9.3.2 The principles of medical audit are the same in all branches of medicine. However the means of carrying it out are bound to differ depending on the nature of the specialty. In particular there are likely to be important differences in the conduct of medical audit between primary care and hospitals partly because of the self-managing status of general practitioners who deal with a very large number of episodes of illness and partly because of the long period of time over which a general practitioner provides primary care. The average time a patient is registered with a general practitioner is 12 years (Difford, personal communication). Longitudinal aspects of care and continuing responsibility are therefore of special relevance. As in medical audit in hospital and community health sectors meetings should take place on a regular basis and careful anonymous records kept.

9.3.3 Since general practice is increasingly adopting an integrated team approach and the process of interdisciplinary work in primary health care is growing steadily there is a need to involve other professionals as well as doctors in medical audit. While medical audit must remain under medical management or supervision this aspect of it must be undertaken and developed sensitively.

9.3.4 While several forms of medical audit are well established in some aspects of primary care medical audit is still a developing concept in others. Individual awareness and participation varies widely. Motivation, trust, education, training and support are essential ingredients to the long term success of medical audit. Motivation is of particular importance in general practice. In order to establish and maintain the necessary level of motivation, the value and contribution of medical audit must be actively promoted. There is a need for strong encouragement and educational initiatives at all levels from medical school, through vocational training and into the practising profession to generate the impetus and motivation required. It is important that the methods of medical audit should be well understood by general practitioners.

9.3.5 The final aim is that by means of an educational approach, medical audit becomes an integral component in the day to day management and clinical care of patients in general practice. The systematic review of patient care is the basis of good future medical practice.

Organization

9.3.6 The FHSA has the responsibility to establish and service locally based audit machinery and needs to be satisfied that there is full local participation producing a responsible outcome. In order to achieve effectiveness, the local professional bodies need to ensure that the format and membership of the Medical Audit Advisory Group (MAAG) should be as indicated in the Health Circular issued by the Department of Health in June 1990[19].

9.3.7 While the FHSA needs to be satisfied that there is a satisfactory range and standard of medical audit being undertaken it is crucial that effective boundaries or 'Chinese walls' exist so that in respect of medical audit confidentiality and professional confidence can be maintained in the long term.

9.3.8 The FHSA through its MAAG will need to ensure overall participation in audit and provide a local framework to ensure that the needs of all general practitioners are met. However, many general practitioners are already firmly committed to a range of existing audit arrangements, for example those associated with the RCGP, which others may also wish to adopt. It is therefore important that suitable criteria are established locally so that satisfactory alternative schemes can be approved by the FHSA on the advice of the MAAG. This flexibility will maintain a number of important options and avoid the exclusion of important arrangements which already command professional support.

9.3.9 The regular examination of its activities by the practice itself, an internal audit, is central to success. However many doctors, particularly those in small and single handed practices, will wish to work in groups. In many cases it may be administratively and functionally impractical for a single MAAG to co-ordinate the whole of an FHSA's area in which there may be 300 or more general practitioners and 20 of more trainees. Geographic considerations are likely to be paramount. We would therefore expect the most likely grouping for an Advisory Group to cover up to 25 practices lying within a Health Authority District. This would usefully match up with hospital and other activities. Where there is more than one Advisory Group in an FHSA it is expected that each Advisory Group would be separately directly related to its FHSA's MAAG and that the MAAGs would collectively coordinate their activities and share their experiences.

9.3.10 Such groups will probably emerge in a variety of settings, convenient for the general practitioners. Those general practitioners wishing to work in groups should, wherever possible, have a choice, and the FHSA's MAAG's could have a role in facilitating this. While it will remain important that professional colleagues head up audit programmes, it also follows that those doctors selected are likely to be busy and heavily committed people. It follows that, just as in the hospital setting, sufficient trained support staff should be provided by the FHSAs. These 'facilitators' should be used under the direction of the MAAG to work on its behalf. Such staff could provide a level and continuity of support which would be important and not otherwise available.

Resources

9.3.11 To be effective it is essential that general practitioners have enough time to sit down together to review each other's work and to consider carefully how standards of care could be improved.

9.3.12 Crucial to any meaningful medical audit is an adequate supply of accurate information. A feature of general practice is the sheer volume and variety of the clinical data it handles. Within the NHS (except in a few unusually dedicated practices where selected data are identifiable) it is not possible to retrieve information reliably unless the practice is computerised. Some forms of medical audit are impracticable without a computer based system. Computer based information systems will facilitate the process of medical audit and allow the full potential of medical audit to be realised. The recent Department of Health survey[20] shows that about a quarter of practices currently use microcomputers and the number is almost doubling annually at present. Information which will be useful for medical audit is thus rapidly becoming available in increasing amounts.

9.3.13 Finally analysing information and extracting information from records, even computer records, takes staff time and the need for such staff must be recognised if medical audit is to be satisfactorily undertaken.

Education

9.3.14 While the basic conduct and administration of audit in general practice will be a local matter, there is an important central contribution to be made in order to promote, develop and co-ordinate medical audit in general practice. This will rely heavily on the co-ordinated contributions of the RCGP and the GMSC so that the right motivation, education and support reaches all GP's and reflects their wants, need and experiences. These two bodies will need substantial central support in order to cover such a wide canvas, which is much larger and more varied than that relating to other individual specialties.

9.3.15 Medical audit in general practice is within the development stage and on that account there needs to be flexibility in how medical audit is conducted so as to allow it to match the varying backgrounds of practice. Nevertheless reference points need to be established so that comparisons can be made, targets identified and progress assessed. Thus there is a need for a central body to collect, collate and publish a range of audit activities and outcomes as a combined promotional/educational exercise. This material would form a useful basis for a series of protocols developed centrally by the RCGP/GMSC.

9.4 Medical audit in the private sector

9.4.1 We believe that medical audit should be considered as part of normal clinical practice; therefore all doctors, whether in the NHS or in the private sector, should participate in a properly structured medical audit programme. We recognise that existing legislation focuses inspection and registration on inputs such as safety of the hospital environment, staffing levels and equipment, and it does not extend to quality of service provided. While health authorities, as the registration and inspection authorities, have power to cancel registration if premises are used for improper or undesirable purposes they have no power to intervene in matters concerning the quality of clinical services.

9.4.2 We do not consider it appropriate that legislation be introduced requiring the private sector to have medical audit in place, as this would go against the essential nature of medical audit as an educational tool in which doctors should take part in a spirit of enquiry and could lead to formal, rigid protocols or procedures in a field where judgement is required. We anticipate that the private sector's desire to develop and maintain high standards of clinical practice will nevertheless encourage medical audit. Health authorities will be able to attach such conditions as they think appropriate to any contract they place with the private sector. We therefore recommend that all NHS contracts placed with the private sector will include a requirement that full and effective medical audit systems are in place.

9.4.3 The pilot audit and accreditation scheme of the Royal College of Pathologists will include assessment of a private pathology department. We understand that a number of private pathology departments and laboratories have expressed an interest in taking part in this scheme and this development is commended.

9.4.4 We note that all BUPA and AMI hospitals have enrolled in the National Confidential Enquiry into Peroperative Deaths (NCEPOD).

10 OUTCOME INDICATORS

10.1 As referred to earlier (para 4.3) Donabedian described the distinction between structure, process and outcome when assessing the quality of health care. Structure was defined as the staffing and facilities in which care takes place together with the organisational and financial arrangements for delivering the care. Process was concerned with what medical care had been applied. Outcome was the result of medical care assessed in terms of survival, recovery and restoration of function. Process measures are more readily available than those of outcome and this explains why historically process has been used more often than outcome to judge quality of care. This has been justified by the assumption that 'good' medical care of known effectiveness has been applied rather than the determination of whether an intervention is beneficial or not in the long term.

10.2. Recently the need to develop outcome indicators has become more pressing, owing to the increasing demand for health care in the face of limited resources and the consequent need to decide priorities in the allocation of resources. Development of outcome indicators has been slow despite considerable research over the past 10 years and the availability of a large amount of data collected routinely on a national basis.

10.3 A major difficulty in the development of outcome indicators has been the collection of relevant data on a national basis. Existing indicators of the quality and outcome of health care are few and more work on them is needed. The recent Korner reports on Health Services Information are now being implemented. Although they are mainly concerned with providing information for NHS management rather than information needed by health professionals to evaluate the results of their care the Korner data can nevertheless provide a useful basis for the development of some outcome indicators.

10.4 Outcome indicators based on routine data include 'avoidable deaths'[21] and some avoidable morbidity indicators such as the rate of admission for diabetic ketoacidosis and coma[22] and readmission rates to hospital following surgery. However, the range of indicators that can be derived from routine data is necessarily restricted, owing to the limited range of data collected.

10.5 A range of outcome indicators is also available from OPCS, relating to preventive services (congenital malformation, infections, cancer, accidents, suicide), treatment services (adverse effects, case fatality, survival data from cancer registries) and overall measures of health (expectation of life, mortality patterns and morbidity patterns from general practice). These data can provide a useful spur for the medical profession to examine current practice.

10.6 Caution is needed in the interpretation of these indicators to take into account factors such as the validity of the data, variations in the incidence and prevalence of disease in the community being served, and other confounding factors including casemix. Their use in carrying out medical audit is therefore limited. There is a need therefore for the profession to identify those areas where the outcome of health service intervention can be used as an indicator of the quality of care. It is important that these areas should be agreed by the profession itself. Of necessity this means that such areas and appropriately defined outcomes should be agreed by the Royal Colleges, Faculties and clinical medical associations for use in medical audit.

10.7 The determination of outcome will often require information about progress of patients whether after discharge from hospital or following treatment in the community. It will be essential to have mechanisms which facilitate follow-up of patients. This could be achieved through the more assiduous use of the NHS number which is currently used on all general practitioners' records and may feature on many personal health records.

REFERENCES

1. Working for patients – Working Paper no 6. Command 555. HMSO 1989.

2. Department of Health and Social Security. United Kingdom reports on confidential enquires into maternal deaths 1985–87 and 1988–90.

3. Royal College of Physicians of London. Medical audit. A first report – What, why and how? 1989.

4. Buck N, Devlin HB and Lunn JN (1987). The report of a confidential enquiry into perioperative deaths. The Nuffield Provincial Hospitals Trust and Kings Fund for Hospitals.

5. Royal College of General Practitioners 1985a. What sort of doctor? Royal College of General Practitioners 1985b. Assessing quality of care in general practice. London, RCGP.

6. Royal College of Surgeons. Report on medical audit.

7. Donabedian A (1966). Evaluating the quality of medical care. Millbank Memorial Federation of Quality. Part 3, no 166–203.

8. Fowkes FGR, Hall R, Jones JH et al (1986). Trial of strategy for reducing the use of laboratory tests. Br Med J *292*: 883–5.

9. Martin AR, Wolf AM, Thibodeau LA et al (1980). A trial of two strategies to modify the test-ordering behaviour of medical residents. N Eng J Med *303*: 1330–6

10. Kincaid WH (1984). Changing physician behaviour: the peer data method. Quality Review Bulletin August: 238–42.

11. Grol R, Mokkink H, Schellevis F (1988). The effects of peer review in general practice. J R Coll Gen Prac *38*: 10–13

12. Fleming D, Lawrence M (1983). Impact of audit on preventive measures. Sr Med J *287*: 1852–1854

13. Gruer R, Gunn AA, Gordon DS, Ruckley CV (1986). Audit of surgical audit. Lancet *1*: 23–6.

14. McClement JW, Howard EH, Mowat AP (1985). Results of surgical treatment for extra-hepatic biliary atresia in the UK 1980–1982. BMJ *290*, 345–347.

15. Mieli-Vergani, Portman, Howard ER, Mowat AP (1989). Late referral for biliary atresia – missed opportunities for effective surgery. Lancet *1*, 421–423.

16. Sellu, (1986). Audit: its effect on the performance of a surgical unit in a district general hospital. Hosp Health Serv Review *82*: 64–9.

17. Shaw C (1989). Medical audit – a hospital handbook. King's Fund Centre, London.

18. Public health in England. The report of the committee of inquiry into the future development of the public health function. Command 289. HMSO 1988.

19. Health Circular on Audit in Primary Care HC(FP)(90)8.

20. Computers in General Practice. Survey by Statistics and Management Information Division. Department of Health 1989.

21. Charlton JRH, Hartley RM, Silver R, Holland WW (1983). Geographical variation in mortality from conditions amenable to medical intervention in England and Wales. Lancet, *1*, 691–696.

22. Lakhani A (1985). Application of outcome indicators in the NHS – a conceptual framework. Paper given at a seminar at Guy's Hospital London June 1985.

Appendix 1

Standing Medical Advisory Committee

Working Group on the Quality of Medical Care

Membership

Sir Eric Stroud (Chairman)

Dr J G Ball

Prof D Pereira Gray

Prof D N S Kerr

Dr J N Lunn

The Lord McColl

Prof D K Peters

Dame Rosemary Rue

Prof J R Salaman

Sir Dilwyn Williams

Dr R Skinner (Medical Secretary)

Mr S Moore (Administrative Secretary)

Dr D Macpherson — Observer (Department of Health)

Dr C Fleming — Observer (Scottish Home and Health Department)

Printed in the United Kingdom for HMSO.
Dd.0293296, 10/90, C920, 3385/4, 5673, 123477.